The Story of Esther

Author: Daniel Malichi

Hi, I'm Esther, join me, as I share my incredible journey of courage and faith. From an orphan to the queen of Persia, I faced adversity with unwavering determination, ultimately saving my people from destruction. Discover the power of hope, forgiveness, and standing up for what is right in this timeless tale of strength and resilience.

© 2024 Daniel Malichi

Hi Everyone, it's me, Esther, yes the famous one from the Bible. Let me tell you my incredible story of courage and how I became queen to save my people.

I lost my childhood innocence forever when my parents' lives were tragically cut short, leaving me an orphan with a lifetime of struggles ahead.

However, I had an amazing uncle called Mordecai. He was so caring and I was lucky enough to be raised by him. He taught me to be strong and brave.

I found myself in the vast Persian Empire, a place filled with luxury and power.

One day, I learned that the Queen had passed away, and a search was underway for a successor. Mordechai urged me to seize the opportunity to make a name for myself, and I decided to throw my hat into the ring by applying for the position.

> Out of all the women of Persia, I was chosen amongst many beautiful maidens to be presented before King Achashverosh.

Through Gods devine control of the world, the King Achashverosh chose me to be the new queen of Persia. I couldn't believe it! I went from being an orphan to a queen in a heartbeat.

At first, I didn't understand why I rose to such power. I didn't know that there was a special reason that I needed to become the Queen of persia.

However, it started becoming clear when the evil man called Haman, who was an influential noble, devised a wicked plan to annihilate my people, the Jews.

Haman devised this plan all because my uncle Mordecai didn't want to bow to him. He was such a power seeker it was revolting.

Mordecai told me that I must do something risky and approach the king uninvited. This idea of his was punishable by death. He told me to ask the king to save the Jews at once. At first, I said to Mordecai, "But I might die if I do this."

However, he quickly responded, "You can save yourself now, but the Jews will be saved another way. But one thing is for certain: your name will be wiped out from all the history books." He recommended that I do as he said, so that my name would be remembered forever.

I went before the king, risking everything, to ask for mercy for my people. King Achashverosh listened and agreed to help. He even honored Mordecai for his loyalty.

I invited the king and Haman to a special feast. At the feast, I revealed Haman's evil plan, and the king was furious. Justice would soon be served.

With the king's support, I issued a new decree, granting the Jews the right to defend themselves against their enemies. The tables were turning in our favor.

The Jews fought back and emerged victorious. We celebrated our deliverance with joy and gratitude. I knew that God's hand was guiding us every step of the way.

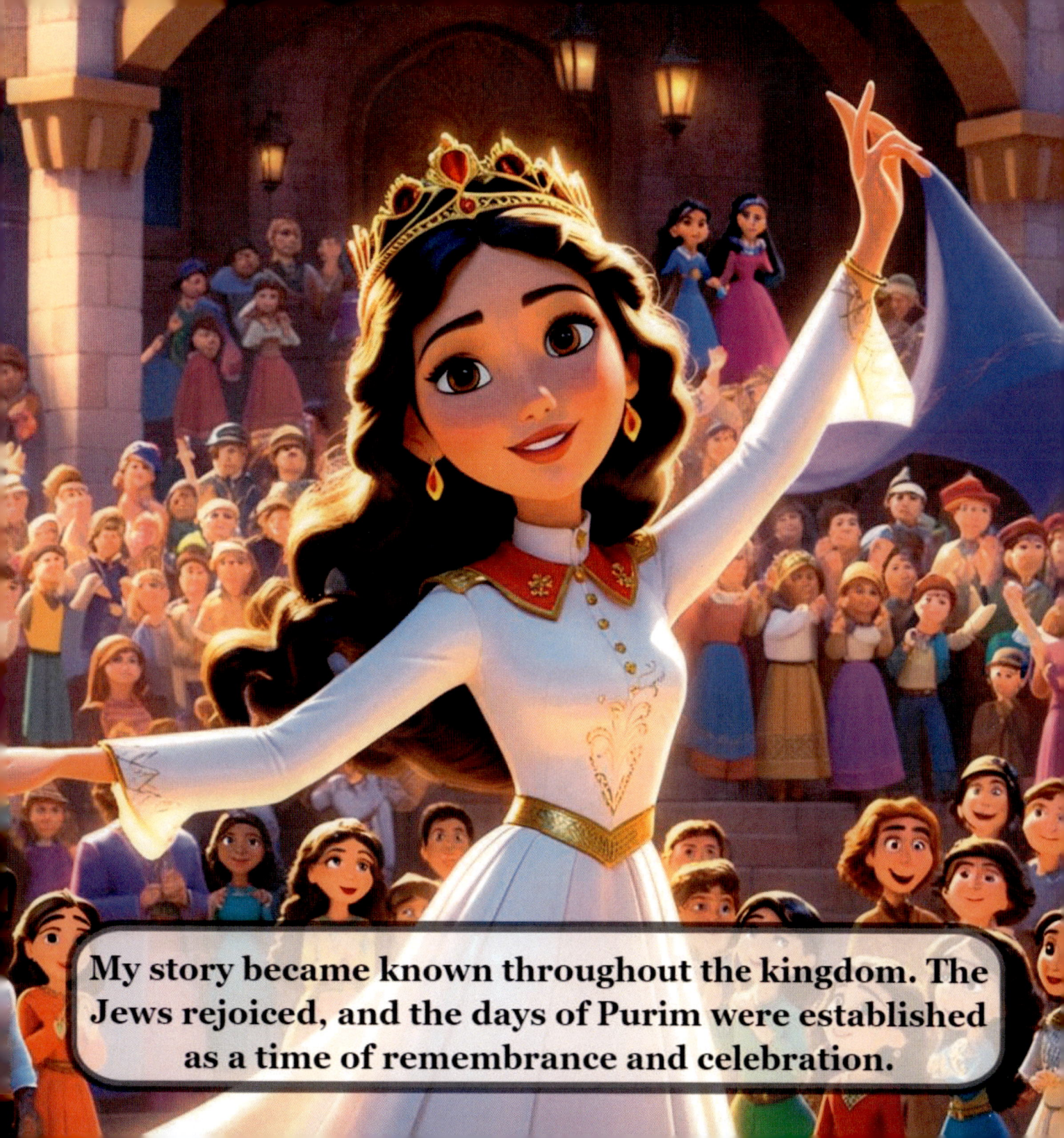

My story became known throughout the kingdom. The Jews rejoiced, and the days of Purim were established as a time of remembrance and celebration.

My story taught others about courage, faith, and standing up for what is right. It is a reminder that even in the darkest of times, there is always hope.

I shared my story with others, inspiring them to be brave and trust in God's plan. I encouraged all to have faith and be a light in the world.

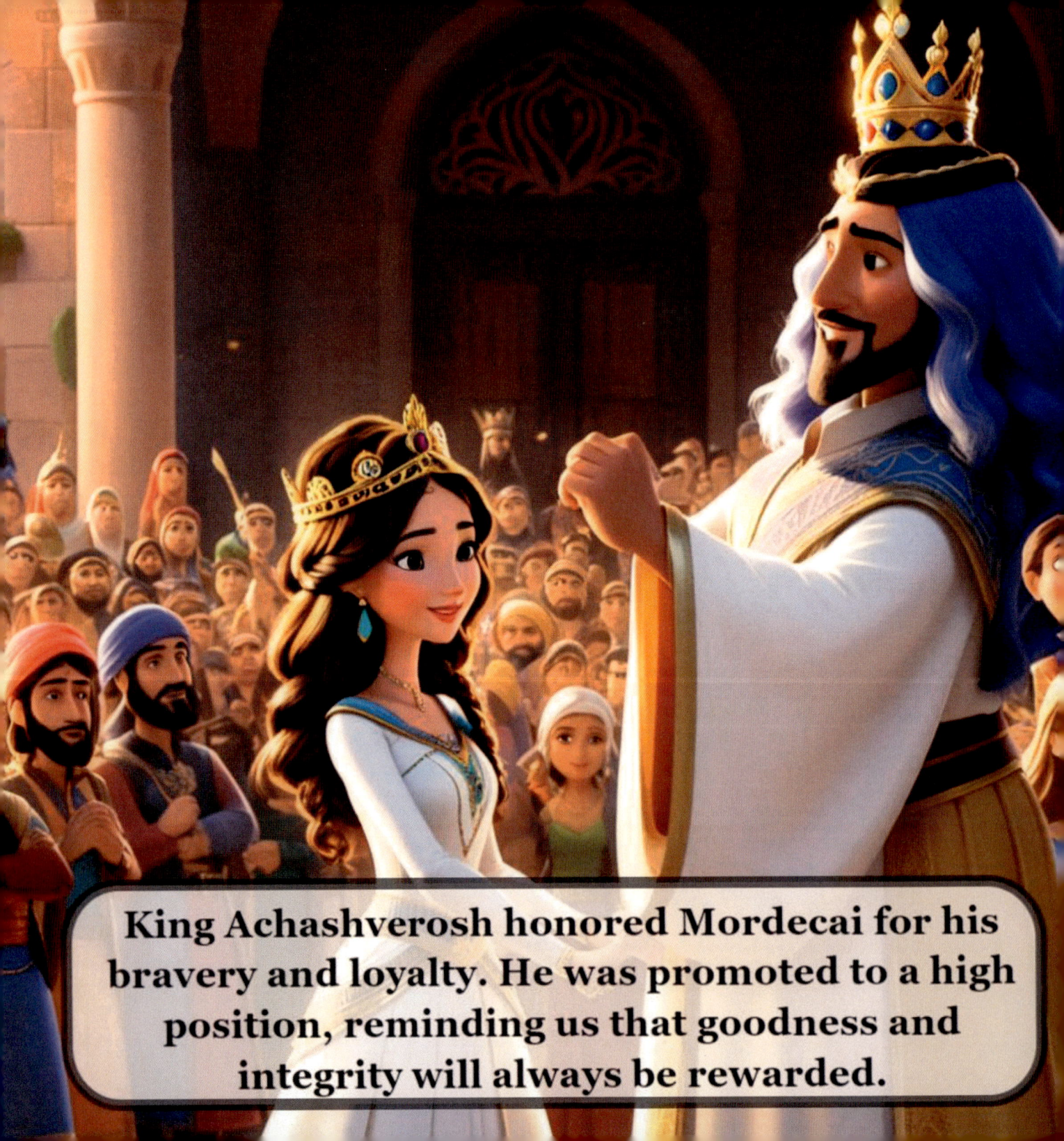

King Achashverosh honored Mordecai for his bravery and loyalty. He was promoted to a high position, reminding us that goodness and integrity will always be rewarded.

I looked back on my journey, from being an orphan to becoming queen, and I realized that every step was a part of a greater plan. I am forever grateful.

I thanked God for guiding me, and for the love and support of my cousin Mordecai. I knew that without them, I would not have had the strength to fulfill my purpose.

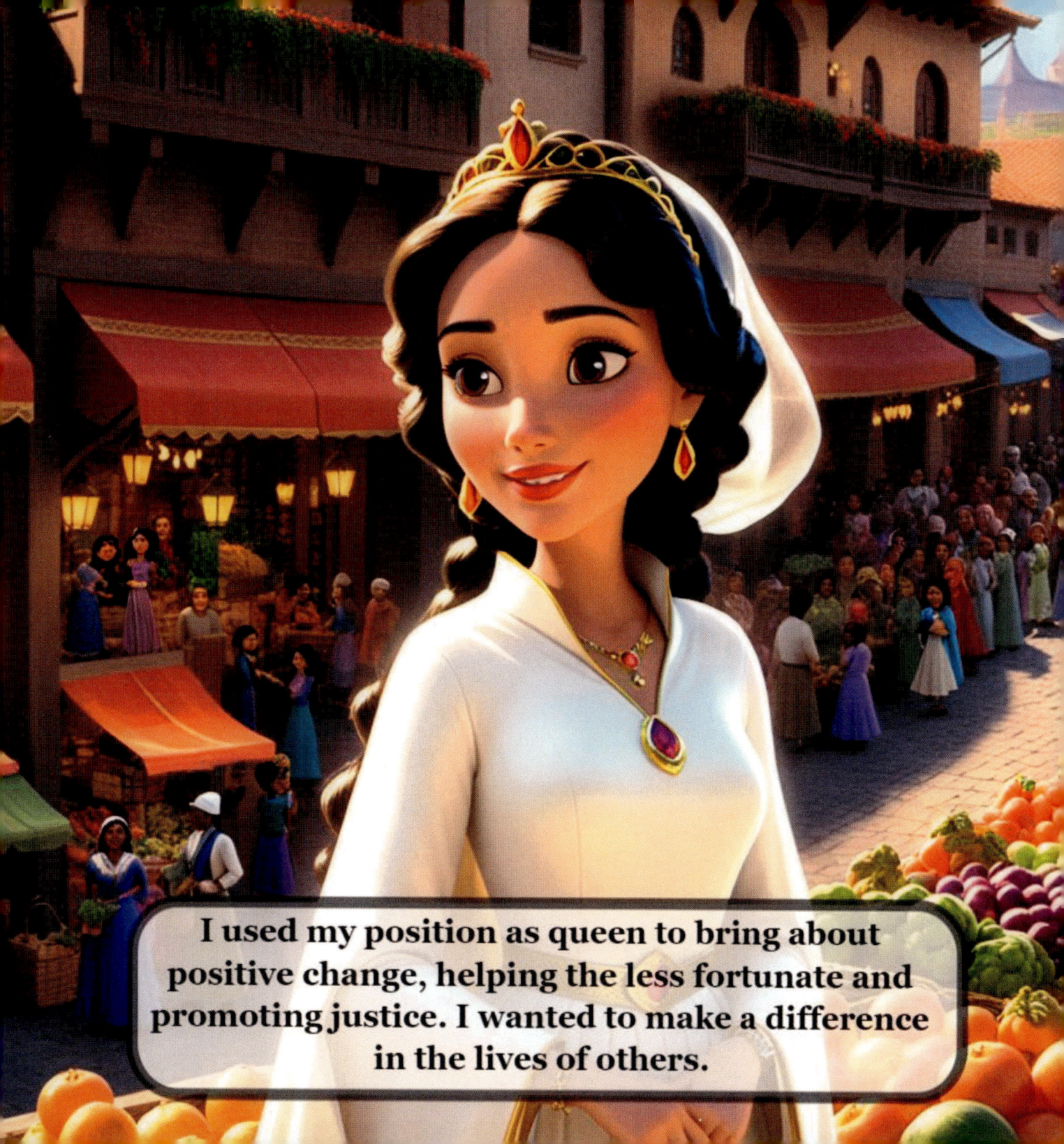

I used my position as queen to bring about positive change, helping the less fortunate and promoting justice. I wanted to make a difference in the lives of others.

My story reminded people of the beauty and power of unity. Jews from all walks of life came together to defeat their enemies and protect their community.

As I ruled alongside King Achashverosh, I worked hard to build a better future for my people. I wanted them to live in a world filled with peace, prosperity, and freedom.

> Through all the challenges I faced, I never gave up. I stood tall and fought for what I believed in. I showed the world that even a young girl can make a difference.

My time as queen came to an end, but my legacy lived on. I knew that my story would inspire generations to come and remind them of the power of faith and courage.

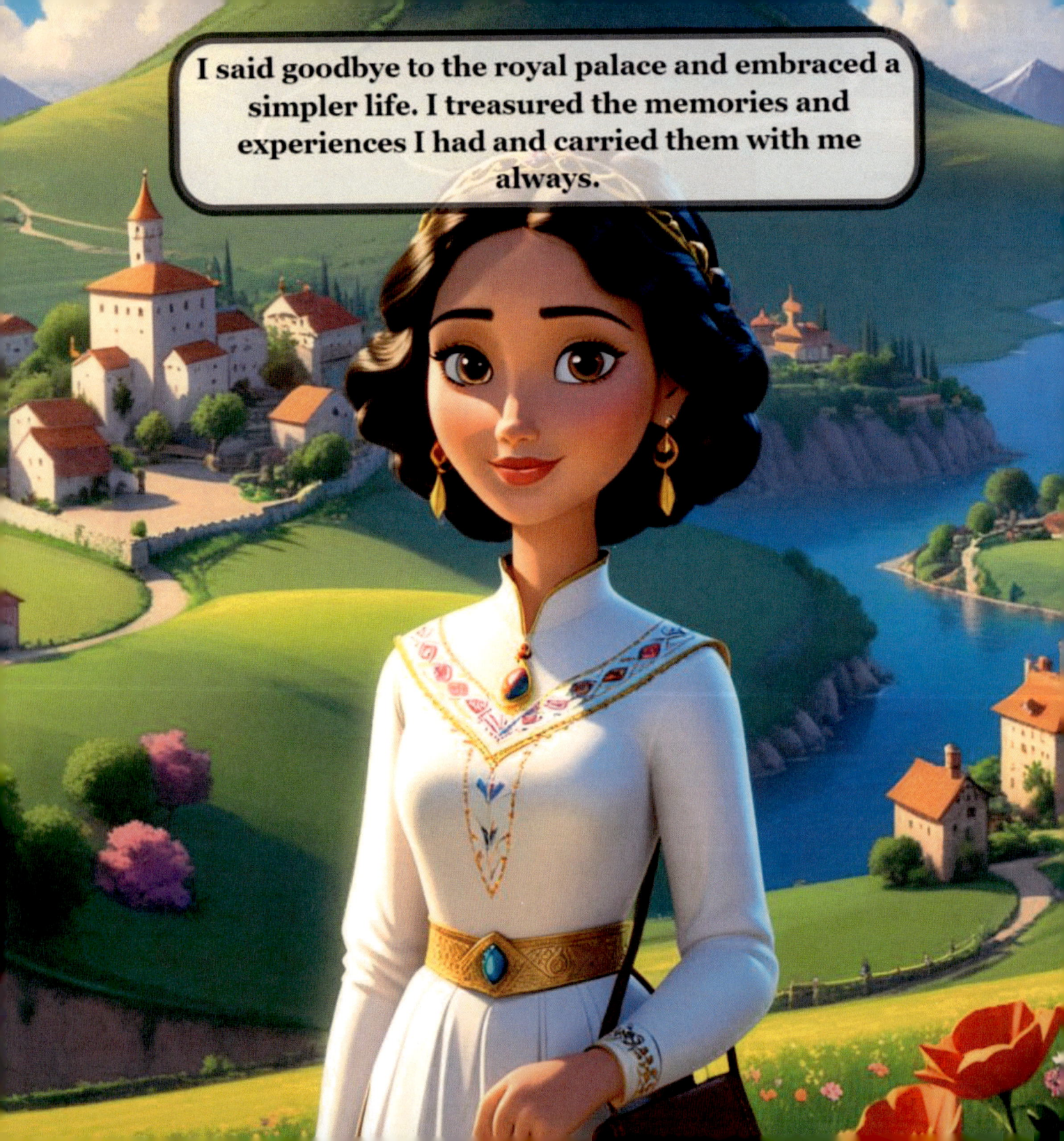

I said goodbye to the royal palace and embraced a simpler life. I treasured the memories and experiences I had and carried them with me always.

People continued to tell my story, passing it down from generation to generation. It became a symbol of hope, reminding everyone that no matter their circumstances, they too can be brave.

My story taught me the importance of believing in myself. I discovered that I had the courage within me all along, and I encouraged others to find their own inner strength.

Faith was at the core of my journey. I relied on God's guidance and trust in His plan. I urged others to seek faith and trust God's timing in their own lives.

I realized that my purpose was so much greater than I could have ever imagined. God had chosen me for a specific mission, and I was determined to fulfill it.

I learned the power of forgiveness, even towards those who had done me wrong. Forgiveness brings healing and freedom, and I encouraged others to embrace it in their lives.

I used my platform as queen to speak up for those who couldn't speak for themselves. I fought for justice and equality, bringing hope to the oppressed.

Even in the face of adversity, I held onto hope. Hope gave me strength to overcome any challenge and inspired others to never give up on their dreams.

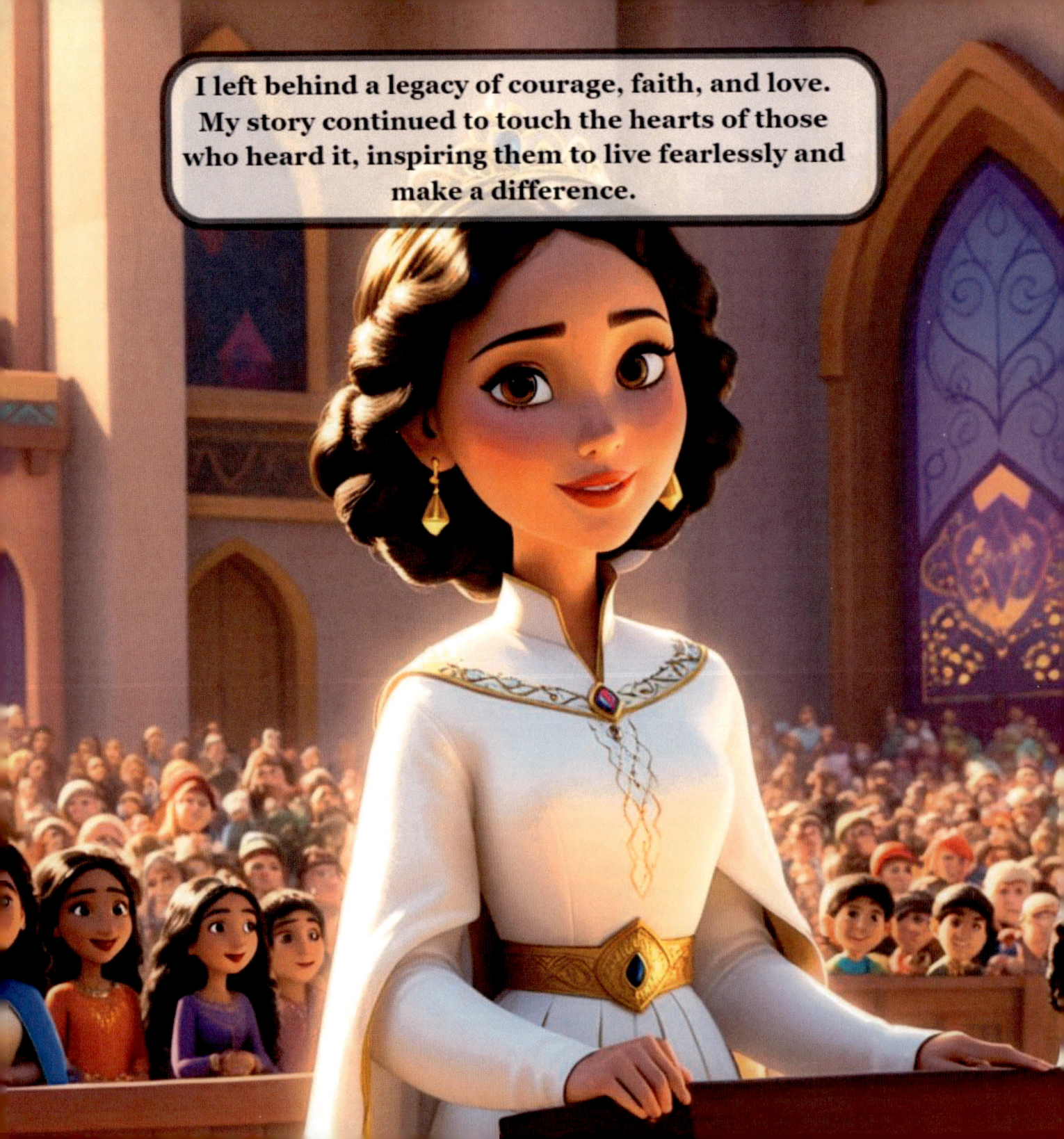

I left behind a legacy of courage, faith, and love. My story continued to touch the hearts of those who heard it, inspiring them to live fearlessly and make a difference.

I thanked God for His faithfulness and for guiding me through every step of my incredible journey. I will forever be grateful for the blessings He bestowed upon me.

My story lives on, reminding future generations to be brave and stand up for what is right. It continues to inspire people to make a difference and change the world.

As time went on, I knew that my time on earth was coming to an end. I bid farewell to those I loved, knowing that my legacy would endure.

People honored my memory, keeping my story alive in their hearts. They celebrated the courageous girl who became queen and saved her people.

Though my earthly journey may have ended, my spirit remained alive. My story is a reminder that the end is just the beginning, and there is always more to come.

Thank you for listening to my story, I was Esther, Farewell for now!